BETTER THAN
The Best
American Poetry

Dave Newman

ROADSIDE PRESS

Cover Art: Lou Ickes
Foreword: David Conrad
Editor: Michele McDannold

Roadside Press
Colchester, IL

Table of Contents

Let Us Now Praise...

Full disclosure, I drink in Dave Newman's house. At his table. Alongside his wife, Lori Jakiela, who he loudly proclaims is the better poet and human – notions she does and does not dispute. They ply me with food and alcohol. They feed me like I'm at a church fundraiser, one with a bar that's open till 3 a.m. A kind of Pittsburgh heaven. Sometimes we take old furniture and burn it in the backyard with the cardboard Dave's too lazy to take to the recycler. We praise poets and singers. We shed a few tears and occasionally Dave kisses me on the mouth.

So, as you can surely tell, I am free of bias.

I say all this not to distract you from Dave's book of poetry but to enforce its central theme: we live in a world of people and things, not in a world where ideas or theory are more important than the people and the things. Words live on the page and in the voice, but people live on the street and in each other's arms.

"No ideas but in things," William Carlos Williams said. And poems are things that add up to sound and song and story, which sometimes glow and rage and make us cry. They don't add up to social justice. As my lovely HS calculus teacher, E. William Turley, once told me, "David, if you really want to make money, go work in a bank." If I sound like David Mamet, I am almost sorry. And the hard and horrible and gorgeous truth is you still have to be able to make beauty to be an artist. You have to be brilliant at your craft.

Clearest example: there is no idea of good music – there is no idea of a good song. There it is. Or it isn't. Same with a poem. It is "beauty bare". A thing reduced to an essence. That we can cherish. And we used to find poets out in the streets, in the bars, in the city, all of us in the gutter, some of us looking at the stars. And if you think I'm quoting Oscar Wilde, I am not. I'm quoting Chrissie Hynde.

So when did we start looking for poets in the halls of academia or on the committee board?

Why are poems now things that have to be explained to the public?

"Mr. Frost what does this poem mean?"

"Well, if I could have said it any more clearly I would have."

Or – and let me quote the man we've gathered here to read – when did we take "an American outsider art filled with rebels and working class folk and turn it into a PG film"?

When did we start to reward kids for poems "made of jargon and shame"?

When did we forget "there are poems so true they should be called knives"?

Or that sometimes...sometimes... poetry, as Charles Bukowski said, "is more important than beans with garlic"?

Okay that's a load of shit, nothing anyone ever wrote is more important than beans with garlic if you're hungry and unemployed.

You only have to read Steinbeck to know that!

"No ideas but in things," William Carlos Williams said about thinking, even though he knew poems are both ideas and things, but still. The poems he wrote, the ones we love and go on loving, glowed and raged and made us cry and love one another.

So much depends upon a red wheelbarrow.

So much depends upon us.

Upon the poets among us.

Then. Now.

But I'm talking about Dave Newman, descendant of Bukowski, fellow consumer of beans with garlic, a Pittsburgh poet who, like his beloved Whitman, contains multitudes the way his hometown contains in its undulating fractal landscape the essence of the working American experience.

And by that I mean what most of us experience.

Let's give Newman space here to define that.

Newman's world is a world where "You can only fill a kid with so much debt and anxiety before they want to walk the bridge to nothingness."

Newman's world is one "Where you need a job to be alive without guilt, where it feels like you're casting bullets to shoot at your own face."

It's our world, the one we know, "Where you're happy every moment you're allowed happiness."

This is a "World that looks like a jail until someone offers words," and where "the world outside never rhymed."

If this is a world that feels like the world you know, thank god you're holding this book in your hands. Maybe it will shine a light for you, the way poet and teacher Toi Derricotte once shone a light for a young Dave Newman. She sent him to an Oakland bookshop with a map to pull down volume after volume of work by poets she knew would speak to him, the way the Old Testament once shouted into the ears of the newly converted. Maybe, in this book you're holding now, you'll find what Dave Newman found years ago – guides, deliverance, the right words, the words from writers who spoke from and for the world he lived in. Maybe you, too, will follow these words like trains rolling down tracks to some distant, true light.

I hope you'll rock with the rhythm of those word-trains, too, and that they'll pull you forward, full of longing and desire, to a destination that rings true to your life and the lives of everyone you know.

And don't forget to burn some furniture along the way. Send up some light into the darkness. As Newman's poems show us, we need that most of all.

–David Conrad, Actor

What is it all for, this poetry,
The bundle of accomplishments
Put together with so much pain?
Do you remember the corpse in the basement?
What are we doing at the turn of our years,
Writers and readers of the liberal weeklies?
–Kenneth Rexroth

I'll bet not one of you has the guts
to yank a page out of the Holy Bible
when you run out of toilet paper
–Nincanor Para

...the heart endures
all bullshit,
the heart endures
right through the final beat
–Bart Solarczyk

For Joe Shields – songwriter, poet, and publisher.
Thank you.
Thank you.
Thank you.

The Poetry Place

I wanted to tell you I'm writing in form.
It's what poets do, they announce forms
in case you don't notice them
which is to say you didn't praise
the poet enough for writing in form.
This is a line about yay long.
This line is a little longer than that line.

Welcome to fuckheadville.

PART 1

Better Than *The Best American Poetry*

Sam Jones teaches writing at Harvard and writes
like an Ivy League degree made of compromise.
Misha LaRoche teaches writing at Columbia and heads
up a committee that counts the number of men
and women published in big-name magazines
to make sure women are properly represented.
Apparently, she never bothered to count
the number of professors those magazines publish
vs. retail-working poets of all genders.
No construction workers. No plumbers. No servers.
Apparently, intersectional feminism is not that intersectional.
You can study with her at a private college in New York
for $63,000 a year or as we call it in my world: a house.
Samantha Hiller teaches at the University of Michigan.
Her student Major Grant edits poems for *The New Yorker*.
He's in here too, with a dog poem that's maybe a cancer poem.
Matt Hampton is a librarian but he has a poem in here
except under the pseudonym Yi Linn, which he sent
out under his own name 40 times before it got accepted.
A famous Indian poet picked the librarian's poem.
He said "I am a brown-skinned poet who gave a better
chance to another supposed brown-skinned poet
because of our brownness" and everyone nodded until
an Indian chick accused him of being a sexual harasser.
Matt Hampton as Yi Linn's poem sucked donkey dick
but so does most of *The Best American Poetry* anthology.
Somehow, universities and the poetry business
have taken an American outsider art filled with rebels
and working-class folks and turned it into a PG film.

No explicit sex, no booze for love, no cheating
on anyone in any relationship ever. It's born-
again Christian stuff masking itself as progress.
Cancel *The Best American Poetry* and the worst thing
that happens is someone doesn't get tenure at a university.

Richard Gegick is not in *The Best American Poetry*.
He owes 100 grand in student loans and the last
time he saw his poetry professor in a restaurant
she either didn't recognize him or ignored him
even though Gegick was handing her wine and food
because he waits tables and writes poems about it.
The alternative newspapers in Pittsburgh
didn't bother to review his book because they
were reviewing books by professors and books
on Big 5 Publishing Houses and university presses.

The fundamental truth of American Poetry is that
once you retire from teaching and your students
quit reviewing your books and interviewing you
on *The Rumpus*, your books die and you end up
banished to eat sushi and complain about poetry
but at least you were able to afford that second
apartment in Brooklyn because it's easier to write
poems when your neighbor is made of money
and answers with quotes made of jargon and shame.

Years ago I got this great handjob at a massage parlor
in McKeesport, an old mill town just outside of Pittsburgh.
The masseuse was older than my mom with a smile
to challenge the sun and skills to sell salt to the drowning.

She was from Vietnam and had been in America
since 1971 after she married a GI for citizenship
then ditched him for the life she'd dreamed to make
for herself since she was doing laundry for pennies.
She owned the place and the first night I showed up
I was drunk and scared and wasn't even sure this
was a sex shop or if it was really a fitness center
with equipment borrowed from another decade.
She stripped me naked and said "You want fuckie?"
which I definitely did not but she pressed and I squirmed
and she bullied, but sweetly, sometimes poking my naked
chest, sometimes touching my cheek like we were lovers
until we negotiated a compromise on a jerkjob for 30 bucks.
There was oil and sexy words and a lot of kindness.
I came back again. I came back again. We got to be pals.
She told me stories about soldiers and war and sex
and love and compromise and bitterness and love.
One time I paid 100 bucks to fuck her and she told me
her grandson was studying to be a dentist and that
        she was paying his tuition.

Beautiful American Songs

He said "You really must read Neruda in Spanish."
If I learned every language of every poet I loved
I'd never have the time to read any poetry, and the
hole in my head would be the size of the midday sun.
Neruda sings to me the way Neruda sings to me.
I like it, and it doesn't take a doctorate to know that.
He said "English just doesn't capture the music."
Okay. I understand that we're a country of racecar
drivers, football fans, crooked politicians, and rock
n' roll reporters, but tell me that you don't love the
sound of your own voice. Tell me that the word
poontang isn't, in its beautiful American way, a song?

A Birthday Poem for Myself

I think I would like to be sucked today.

If you were thinking flowers, please stop.

There is something about your face
        that makes me hard.

If you were thinking a gift card
        make it for my cock.

Whatever else, I'll take head.

Lick the tip for breakfast, my balls for lunch.

I hope to come in your mouth for the whole day.

Too much of this world is filled
with things that are not your lips and my cock.

Happy birthday to me!

May my dick be the candle you love to blow.

Correspondence Courses, Maps, and Other Means of Stimulation

You husbands should take a correspondence course
if you don't have the courage to do it in person
on the female genital organs
-Nicanor Parra

Maybe all men should take
a correspondence course
what with people waiting until
much later to get married.
Maybe we should be issued
feelers and longer tongues.
Maybe our hearts should
grow to the size of tall
buildings and we should leap
over premature ejaculation
in a single bound. Maybe
we should start a petition
to make the word vagina
illegal. Maybe sexy body
parts shouldn't sound like pasta.
Maybe guys are scared to go
down on a gemelli or a campanelle.
Maybe the chorus of every
pop song should sing pussy
and we should all hum it together.
Maybe the committee should issue
a recall on mean nasty women.
Maybe women should go in
for their own tune-ups.

Maybe women should write
the book. Maybe women
should read the book too.
Maybe men don't have time
for the correspondence course.
Maybe it's a bad idea. Maybe
we all shouldn't fuck the same.
Maybe we should all fuck
as well as we want to fuck.
Maybe we shouldn't fuck at
all. Or we should fuck all day.
Everyday. With everyone we know.

At the very least, I propose that
we issue a map to all the interested
parties, a sort of general overview of
how things work, a diagram with
directions and pictures, arrows, hearts
and gold stars, like the drawing I did
for my freshman roommate who dated
the same girls for two years
and had no idea where the clit was.

For Frank O'Hara

I don't ever want to get run over by a dune buggy and die.
Frank O'Hara loved the Surrealists but not that much.
I'm indifferent to the Surrealists but I love Frank O'Hara.
If you have to die, go with the dune buggy.
I'm the age now that Frank O'Hara will always be
but my liver is in better shape and I'm still writing.
This is all so dreary but Frank knew poetry was fun.
Sometimes I go to the museum not to look at the paintings
but to think of Frank O'Hara working behind the counter.
Frank O'Hara does not work at the counter of the museum
I visit so I look at the paintings. I've been working
on this poem for nine days and it's not close to finished.
I've been working on this poem for years so I can keep
re-reading Frank O'Hara and wandering the museum.
O'Hara wrote his poems on scraps of paper and postcards.
Publishers dug the poems from his pockets and bags.
You can put anything in a poem as long as it's fun.
You can put anything in a poem as long as it's true.
I don't trust anyone who composes hammered except
when I trust the final composition. Poems are not paintings.
You can't fling words like paint on the canvas of the page.
Frank O'Hara got laid a lot and everyone loved him.
I love him from a distance. I disagree with everything
he ever said about poetry except the poems he wrote.
Take form. O'Hara said "If you're going to buy
a pair of pants you want them to be tight enough
so everyone will want to go to bed with you."
Frank O'Hara wanted to be a painter, not a poet.

I want to be a poet, not a painter. It's America
that makes us great even when we sometimes hate America.

I hope to get laid on the night I die.

Frank O'Hara Frank O'Hara Frank O'Hara.

PART 2

Wilmerding, Pennsylvania, Thinking of Fred Voss

The houses are being foreclosed on
but the kids are still in the streets
playing with chalk, riding bikes

and the old men sit outside a café
drinking coffee, waiting for the bars

and I am walking here
because I have been unemployed
      for two months
      and what I can afford
      is the YMCA
      to lift some weights
      or swim
then walk the cracked sidewalks outside

and I remember reading Fred Voss' poems
      in my tiny apartment
      when I was 21 or 22
      all those wonderful lines
      about working as a machinist
      up and down the coast
      of California and inside
      Goodstone Aircraft Company
      that awful place with sparks
      flying and sharp objects
and bosses welded down to the meanest of hearts

      and I remember thinking:

Jesus, I hope I don't end up like Fred.

How beautifully he wrote!

How hard he worked!

Fred dropped out of a PhD program
      to become a machinist
      but I was going to graduate school
      so I didn't have to work
      with my hands
      because there were no jobs
      working with your hands
      in Western Pennsylvania
          in 1989

      and because my mom
      never made college

      and my dad, a factory worker
      who'd been employed
      since he'd quit school
      in the sixth grade
      to load melons
dreamed better things for his kids
      like becoming
      an engineer
      or an accountant

but definitely not graduate school
      for poetry

but the directions drive us, not vice versa
we end up where we end up, not where we want.

     I wanted to teach college
     but no one liked my poems
     about working as a janitor
     and taking drugs
     and reading
     Nicanor Parra
     in the parking lot
     before work
     with a ham sandwich
     in my lap

and my professors thought I was unintelligent
     not academic
     and / or a heroin addict

     plus I once showed up to a party
     with a three-gallon ball of beer
     and everyone else brought hummus

so I graduated in two years
with the same grades as everyone else.

Most of my peers got jobs teaching
     but I got a job in a warehouse
     where I loaded ball-bearings
     into a truck
     and delivered them
     to factories

and read more poems by Fred Voss
     who was still a machinist
     who is still a machinist
     who is still writing poems

who is the only poet in America
who is the only poet in America

who could have survived
in Wilmerding, Pennsylvania
     circa 1870
     when George Westinghouse
opened the Westinghouse Airbrake Company
and the men worked 55 hours a week
with steel made to stop a locomotive

and I like to think of Fred in the fire
     burning with the men
     who had to burn
     because he wanted to burn
because he knew someone needed to record this—

how practical poetry is in the hands of a machinist
     how you can still build
     your life around poetry
when it's made by people who make things we need.

But it's 150 years after George Westinghouse
     opened the Airbrake plant
     and the black smoke
     looked like clouds
     and prosperity

and now the city is a hologram of itself
      factories looking like factories
      but not doing what factories do

and I have been reading Fred's poems again
      terrified and in awe
      thankful and humbled

but this afternoon, it's 90 degrees
and I have my own work

my heart pumping past the railroad line
      that hauls coal somewhere
      away from Wilmerding, Pennsylvania

where Fred Voss never lived or worked

and a dog on a chain barks vicious
at a torn black garbage bag

and two guys covered with tattoos
head up a ladder, carrying shingles.

The Economy

Despite a busted capillary
which colored one of my eyes

so it looked like a tiny mouse heart
beating in my socket

I felt like mercury
on a glass table: slip slide-y.

Now that I had less
I believed I'd be able to do more.

My brother showed up
wearing dark sunglasses

and a scraggly-ass beard.
He ordered a vodka tonic

then said "You can't be fat
and on coke, it doesn't work."

I considered that
while I finished my drink

turning my mouse heart
to the bright lamp

hanging above the bar
then back down to our conversation.

Drugs were not the issue.
It was employment and opportunity.

My brother said "Seriously"
and took a card from his wallet.

"Nice sunglasses" I said.

You Really Want to Work Here?

I walked into his office and he said "Outside"
so I followed him out back to some dirt

and some guys standing around
and some other guys operating heavy machinery.

He said "Where is Mario?
Did Mario fucking quit too?"

Apparently, quitting was a problem.
I suspected low pay and bad working conditions.

None of the guys standing around
or operating heavy machinery answered.

The rage in the air felt a lot like
the rage in the air everywhere.

The guy from the office said
"You really want to work here?"

He fixed his hair like a barber
made of electricity and bad drugs.

I said "I do" which I didn't
which is what the world of money is about.

He said "Here you go then"
and handed me a shovel.

Eric Miles Williamson

who is a pretty great novelist
and a pretty vicious literary critic

who grew up in a trailer
on the parking lot

of an auto shop
where his dad worked

when he wasn't in prison.
Eric Miles Williamson

who sometimes lived with his mom
who basically fucked bikers for drugs

and would have preferred
that her son go away or die.

Eric Miles Williamson
once said about academics

who preached the virtues
of class-based literature

"For people who love books
about working-class people

they sure don't like it
when one of us is around."

He got one of my books published.
I bought him a bottle of whiskey

on an almost full credit card.

Poem for Charles Bukowski and Anzia Yezierska

Outside, poverty. The smell of the city, trash.
You're born in the ghetto, and your father says
"No woman can live without a father or a husband
to look out for her" or you're born during
the Depression and your father, who can't find
work, beats you with a razor strap until the skin
on your back cracks, bleeds, and your mother
watching, says "The father is always right."
After that, freedom, individuality, the library.
More poverty, endless poverty, a little education
at the city college, maybe a degree in teaching.
At seventeen, you get a job in a laundry, you sell
fish in the streets or you hit the road from LA
to Philadelphia, find jobs in a dog biscuit factory
or Western Union, stockboy at an autoparts store.
What does any of it matter except to say nobody
starved to death and there was always enough paper.
Through spite and through love, the words came.
The class you were born into barely reads, let alone
writes but, suddenly, there were books, stories
and poems, novels, novels about dirty New York
the Lower East Side, books about dirty Los Angeles.
You ironed shirts, you write it into your art.
Eleven years at the Post Office, make it a novel.
There were lovers, children, one daughter each.
The pull and push of family, writing, always family.
In 1927, a jerkwad critic at the *New York Tribune*
said this about Yezierska "a complete and amusing
ignorance of gentile minds, and somehow a faint

lack of good taste." When Bukowski published
his first novel in 1972, *The New York Times*
was too ignorant to notice, too smart to care.

None of it, of course, mattered in the least.

> If I believe in anything anymore
> > it's art
> > it's survival
> > it's the cost
> > of being
> > an individual.

> If I believe in anything anymore
> > it's the cost of finding
> > beauty at all costs.

Anzia Yezierska and Charles Bukowski.

> The world looks like a jail
> until someone offers words.

Etheridge Knight

In ninth grade he said "Fuck this"
and got a job shining shoes.
To shining shoes, he said: fuck this.
The pool hall was a hustle that
barely paid what it offered.
He was one of seven children
in Mississippi. There are blues
so deep, nobody knows.
He bought a drink and didn't stop.
Here's a toast: when the ship goes
down, swim motherfucker!
The government was willing to pay
black kids who were willing to go to war.
The drugs in the jungle were the best.
Home was different. The destination
of America was still unknown.
If he wanted to stay high, he needed crime.
10 to 25 was ridiculous, your honor.
Mistakes were made but not devastation.
James Baldwin said "The bitterness which had
helped to kill my father could also kill me."
It would take a mathematician to write this formula:
race + addiction + crime + incarceration = art.

There are poems so true they should be called knives.

PART 3

A Letter to Amazing

Dear Joan Jobe Smith–

You have the best stories. I sometimes think of my luck, that I know someone who go-go danced at the world-famous Whiskey a Go Go while rockstars did what rockstars did 50 years ago. Jim Morrison drunk, singing Rimbaud. I know you had horrible husbands and no money and kids that needed raised and pecan trees of talent waiting to bloom.

I owe you a letter and plan to write it soon.

We've known each other for more than 20 years and met exactly once. I'm thankful and sad. I wish we'd been rich and drank champagne at breakfast.

When I was a senior in college, I lived in a transient motel in Irwin, just off Route 30. I had a couple jobs and lived on noodles and booze. I ate stress like candy and dreamed poetry was a house I'd build and that house would be made of enough money to allow me to create art. But I knew it was bullshit. I looked like a landscaper and sometimes worked as a landscaper. I stole a lot and felt embarrassed for stealing because I read so much. I worked so much. My face looked like a whiskey bottle. My face looked like a whiskey bottle made of broken glass. I spilled everywhere. I read poetry every second, every minute. My apartment was one room and a bathroom. The couch was a bed but I mostly slept on the floor. I got laid a lot from a crazy chick who was rich but sometimes stole money from my wallet. I was fine with that. I read your poems in *The Wormwood Review* about raising kids and crazy husbands and cooking beans and raising kids, kids from all kinds of crazy husbands, so many poems, all of them brilliant. I wrote to someone who knew you had a book on Event Horizon Press and somehow I found Event Horizon's phone number and called to order your first book, which seemed inconceivable, a first book, only one book, because I'd read so many of your brilliant poems that I assumed you were a god made of poetry and wisdom.

I gave the publisher my credit card number over the phone.

He said "Can you give me those again?"

I did.

He said "It's not going through for some reason."

The reason was because I'd paid for all my textbooks and not made the bill.

I said "I'll send you a money order" and I did.

I waited for a week by the mailbox.

Then I read *Jehovah Jukebox* 3 times the day it arrived and have been reading it ever since. You danced and you sang and you married poorly and you loved Charles Bukowski and Bukowski called you drunk and you drove a VW Beatle and fell over your children to make better lives for them.

I knew you before I knew you.

You married a brilliant poet, Fred Voss, after so many bad men.

I married a poet and gave her your book and she fell in love with your words because she saw your world in her life and our life and all the lives of the men and women she knew. She was a professor but barely, making less than she did as a flight attendant. She took your book to class. She gave it to students. They loved you.

She gave it to her feminist colleague who said "I don't get it."

Fuck her.

Women who claim to write about the body seldom know what the body is or what it costs.

One day, when I was working 60 or more hours a week and dying and trying not to die because I had a son and a wife I loved, I came home from my job and found a letter from you in my mailbox. You'd read one of my stories in a magazine over in England that didn't hate working-class folks. You said so many nice things. It was like getting a letter from a god who loved d.a. levy and fit perfectly in a woman's body. Your handwriting looked like curls made of art.

Years later, we'd hug.

I was probably too embarrassed to say my world would have died if you wouldn't have written, not to me, but your poems.

Thanks, Joan.

I am here because you believed in yourself enough to make art.

I'll get you that letter soon.

I owe you so much more.

Love,
Newman

Phil Levine

He worked in an auto factory in Detroit and went to Wayne State University. I thought poets were supposed to be flouncy and wear blouses. The year I graduated from high school, they closed the auto factory in Western Pennsylvania, and my father moved to Detroit and I went to a place called Slippery Rock University and no one mentioned poetry.

I attended a community college.

I attended another community college.

My father was an electrician. He used his hands and did things with wires that the guys on the line could only dream about doing.

I think Phil Levine dreamed. He dreamed of words and their order. He dreamed of an assembly line in his head where he made books like cars.

The only poetry I had was high school English, meaning Shakespeare. Shakespeare wore a blouse and used a lot of fancy words. I read *Romeo and Juliet* and didn't understand anything, not even love. We watched the movie and Juliet had her tits out so some kids giggled. There's a lot of poetry in tits when you're 16 and hate to read. My father would have worn a blouse to work if it would have helped his son get a good education, get a good job, get a better life.

I read Phil Levine in college and he turned my head like a screw. I didn't see his picture for years. I assumed he wore a blouse and heels.

I hoped he wore grease stains like blush on his cheeks and he clicked his heels before he wrote poems about going back to Detroit.

For years I believed in maps, that you could read someone and about someone, and their life and work would provide direction.

When I told my dad I was going to graduate school for poetry he said "You're kidding me, right?" but he hadn't read Phil Levine and I had and we all know what happens to poor kids who like to read.

Working Class

Every other culture finds rewards
for their suffering.

We are held accountable
for the wealth of the rotten class.

Everyone Loved Drugs but I was the Only One Who Read

There were three of us and we wanted to get fucked up.

Everyone had bank accounts made of chicken wire.

I said "I'll kick in 40 then I'll have 30
        to last the rest of the week."

Math for the seekers adds up like novels:
        detail here, plot point there
        hope the climax
        doesn't destroy us all.

Everyone kicked in 40.

An 8-ball cost $120.

The dealer smoked crack but didn't drink
and he thought he was living the sober life.

No one else would ride with me
        let alone step into his apartment.

He said "There's my poet.
You still pulling daisies?"

I said "You still smoking crack?"

He said "Does it look like the weekend?"
        and reached for his crackpipe

resting at the far edge
of the coffee table
sliding it closer
like the pipe might grow
glass legs and wander off.

An old leather shaving bag
        the kind my dad packed
        for summer vacation
rested in his lap like a brown puppy.

I'd published 20 poems in magazines
        almost no one knew existed.
        The editors worked
        in factories or print shops
        or as go-go dancers
        and the writers they published
        drove cabs and worked
        in factories and restaurants.

I don't know how my drug dealer had discovered
        I was a writer
        but *poet* sounded
        exactly like *bullet*
                the way he chewed it
                in his teeth.

Maybe I'd mentioned I was a poet.
I dreamed a lot about being a poet.
        I sometimes spoke
        without meaning to.

The dealer said
"What we have here
is a failure to communicate"
but he said it smiling
like we were about
to communicate.

He wore his nose like a hand grenade.

He watched old movies and memorized lines.

I thought: if he looks like he's going
to punch me I'm going to punch him first.

I don't mean to sound tough.

I was pretty nervous about the deal
      about crack users
      about writing poems
      no one read.

All my dreams revolved around
      time and money:
      time to read and write
      and money to buy books.

And, between stations, getting fucked up.

I said "You want to snag me an 8-ball?"
and tried to make it sound like: please
      or maybe like:

the customer is always right
or maybe like:
don't shoot me, okay?

He started to open the leather shaving bag
    pulling the zipper slowly
    then yanking
    when the zipper stuck
    then motherfucking
    the zipper
    then abandoning
    the shaving bag
    to fire up his crackpipe
    with a blow torch
    the size of a baby shoe.

"Better?" I said.

"Will be" he said and used
his teeth to open the bag
and the open bag revealed
so many 8-balls of coke.

He said "80 bucks a piece."

Then he said "2 for $150."

He moved like a car salesman
who wanted to lose his commission.

Or he moved like god
inventing a better 7th day.

I said "2 for $150" and pulled out
the money plus the 30 I needed for the week.

So this is the night I learned to read
in a way I'd have to read for years to come.

I loved my friends and when I told them lies
      I barely believed
      they were lies
      and when they handed me
      the extra money
      and thanked me for the drugs
I sat down under the dreams I'd been dreaming.

It was very complex, the way I scammed them.

Who rips off their friends?
      Writers.

Sorry, lie.

Who rips off their friends?
      Poor writers.

I spent the next day in Caliban Books
      far right aisle, poetry section
if you looked through the glass storefront.

I stretched out on my back with a stack of books
      reading
      reading
      reading

trying to decide how many I would buy.

I loved books so much.

Heaven looked like a library, one I'd bought.

Or stolen.

Diane Wakoski

I called her once when she was teaching at Michigan State.
I was 22 years old and working as a janitor.
I thought I'd go to grad school to study books
instead of mops and brooms and dirty toilet bowls.
I was the first person in my family to graduate college.
You could read Diane Wakoski on the job with a broom
in one hand, a book in the other. You didn't have to go
to grad school to understand her poems. I didn't want
to go to grad school to study with Diane Wakoski.
I wanted to go to grad school to get a fucking job.
I wanted to tell her I loved her poems and that maybe
she would love my poems and we could be friends.
I wanted her to tell me I could be a teacher and not
a truck driver made of 18 wheels and no education.
But books are not people and authors are not their books.
Diane Wakoski was cranky on the phone, vaguely disgusted.
She asked for my name 3 times then cleared her throat.
I wondered if she'd ever called William Carlos Williams.
Those are the connections I was able to make at 22 years old.
Diane Wakoski writes like William Carlos Williams but better.
William Carlos Williams was not a crank. He was a doctor.
If you have to call a poet, call one who believes in medicine.
My favorite Wakoski title: *Dancing on the Grave of a Son of a Bitch*.
She knew how to take a lover down in a poem: You ride
a broken motorcycle / You speak a dead language /
You are a bad plumber / You write with an inkless pen.
I sort of wanted to marry her after reading those lines.
I used to fight with women and lose the fights and write about it.
The women that I fought with seldom thought of me as a writer.

One lady slapped me across the face and said "Write about that!"
I wrote about it. I wrote "Your slaps are like wrecking balls
but I am a very large building made of brooms and water."
Diane Wakoski didn't seem to know much about grad school
even though she was in an office at a university.
I said "Well, I really love your poems." She said "Thank you."
I have not spoken to Diane Wakoski since, though I still read her
books. If you see her, tell her "Hello" and I hope she finally retired.

Careerism Vs. Literature

      Years ago
when I was in grad school
I had a poetry professor
who wasn't much of a teacher
but was a lot of fun to drink with.

One evening after a night class
when I'd workshopped a poem
that showed some explicit sex
he pulled me aside and said
      in a very serious way
"I may drink a whole bottle
      of Jack Daniels
      and fall down the stairs
      but it doesn't mean
      I have to put it in a poem"

which may have been decent career advice
and suddenly made clear his own PG-rated poems.

I was writing autobiographical narratives
      like most young poets
and my autobiography was pretty scruffy:

I lived an old apartment with a struggling Army vet
and an undergraduate alcoholic who stood
6 feet tall and sometimes set his hair on fire

I was 3rd assistant manager at B. Dalton

which meant I had to steal dinner money
from the cash registers to have a proper meal

Some nights I worked as a janitor
        the first job I'd found
        out of college

I read and believed Baudelaire when he said
"Be drunk...with wine, virtue, or poetry"
though I would have added dope and fucking
and long mornings staring at the ceiling
        with vigor and great seriousness
and eating long slow breakfasts with bacon
and listening to Bo Diddley at midnight
and tongue kissing strangers in Dee's Bar.

I didn't have insurance and wouldn't for years.

I was a recovering born-again Christian
who woke each morning with God
        puking last night's sins in my ear.

I subsisted on writing and reading
believing that somehow my poverty
        might end up useful.

What my professor meant was: be fake.
        He meant: tell half-truths.
        He meant: have the affair
        but never: put it in a poem.

He could have been everyone I knew
at church and work, the people I'd hoped
to ditch by becoming a serious writer.

My professor put his arm on my shoulder.
The other students walked off, maybe
believing I was receiving extra praise.

What my professor meant was: be bullshit.
        He meant: the way to success
is inaccuracy and a spit-polished life.

I laughed at him, not in a mean way
        but because I was stunned.

The language I most loved and wrote in
was barspeak, dive barspeak, and it may
have sounded garbled in a workshop
obsessed with politics but it told more truth
than anything I'd ever heard in a classroom
and I'd have quit writing before I spoke
in anything less than what I heard in the night.

Do I have to say my professor is more successful
        than I am and ever will be?

        This happened decades ago.
It's still everything that's wrong with literature
and the general fuckheadedness of the world–
no one telling the truth but claiming it's the truth.

Liberals in America

Beware folks who talk about the working class
then shout down the waitstaff over the placement
          of their ranch dressing.

Beware the other people too.

All of them.

Every single fucking one.

Bio Notes

He craps himself. She writes about rape because she secretly thinks it's sexy. She hates men. He hates women. Neither of them acknowledges nonbinary folks because they think it's weird except when they're feeling exceptionally white and vulnerable. He is the Douchebag Professor Emeritus at Douchebag University in Fuckhead, New York. She is the chair of Menstrual Cycle at Cuntbag College. She's fat and likes to call people fat shamers. He's fatter and likes to be shirtless in the summer. Her picture beneath this Bio Note was a glamour shot. It cost two hundred dollars. He made his wife shoot his author photo then shouted her down for how ugly he looked. He wanted to look like David Foster Wallace. In her author photo she wanted to look like Marilyn Monroe. She hates fashion magazines and skinny women. She wishes she was skinny. In 1987, she won the Silicone Boob Award for her poem "My Big Boobs." The National Endowment for the Arts gave her a grant for $25,000. She said "Thank you, America, I didn't know how I was going to afford to get my bathroom remodeled and go to Paris." He visited Paris the previous summer. The wine gave him gas. Wine gives her wrinkles. She hates Paris because Paris did not love her and she regrets her first novel *Paris, My Love*. He flirted with a couple waitresses but they dismissed him as a tourist. He wrote a book of poems called *I'm a Whore for You, Paris* but no one wanted to publish it, not even his university's press. He writes his lectures so his female students think he's sexy. They don't. She hates her female students, those skinny bitches. She once dated a boy grad student but he was nervous and could never get hard. She wrote a book called *The Patriarchy Fails Us All*. He never gets laid and he blames America. In 1992, he was awarded the Most Trying But Least Succeeding Professor To Never Bang A Student Award from the Council for Limp Dick Arts. Last year, he doubly crapped himself at Yaddo and, as a graduate student, studied with Sir Crapsalot at the University of Iowa Writers' Workshop. She studied with a tampon at Oxford.

PART 4

Boat

I'm not going to use the word boat
in this poem unless I'm on a boat
unless I can see a boat on the water
or my neighbor's boat, the white
wood junker he bought for $83
and parked in his driveway
and never refurbished because
he works 60 hours a weeks
doing physical therapy for seniors
and more time than that not being
married and not having children
and not dating and not saying "Hi"
and more time than that being sad.
It's a job, being sad. It will make a man
buy stuff. You can fill your heart with boats
and water and never make the lake, never
make the river, never see the ocean
and other people, people who believe
in metaphor and contextualizing the form
will forget you and steal your boat
and write about your boat as something
else and, also, there will be trees.

Wordsworth

I get it: nature
is beautiful
and sometimes
we all feel like
our hearts
are dancing
with the daffodils.

I sort of wish
you'd been eaten by a bear.

The Right Kinds of Poems

"Your poems contain
too many references to alcohol"
says the woman who writes
poems about trees and her mom
and is never wrong about poetry

as I chug a beer
to calm down

after giving a reading
with a woman who writes
poems about trees and her mom
and is never wrong about poetry

     and
as far as I can tell
may have fucked a tree
     stone-cold sober.

Despite my alcohol-numbed senses
I'm sure I could smell some knotty pine.

I Used to Always See Bouncers

sitting on their stools, reading Bukowski
between checking IDs and knocking heads.

Now they're on their phones.

Angels with Ugly Faces, *or*
The Cover of Gerald Stern's *The Red Coal*
—for Bob Pajich

I can't remember if it was before or after
I took you to Denny's Bar for your 21ˢᵗ birthday

and you drank buttery nipples and large beers
while squeezed between old alcoholic men

who downed large beers and short whiskeys
and marveled at your enthusiasm

but you showed up at my apartment
with the copy of *The Red Coal* you'd borrowed

from the Carnegie Library
with Stern and his pal Jack Gilbert

sharing the cover photo: one shot
of them as old and ugly

and the other shot
of them as young and ugly

and by ugly
I mean Stern – Jack Gilbert

was as handsome
as a movie star

and you were too, Bob
even as my face had already

started to collapse from reading
and writing more than I slept.

I was 24 and believed poetry
was an element no different

than oxygen or carbon
and at least as important

as a ham sandwich
for survival.

So you were finally legal
and hugged the whole bar

then stumbled back to my apartment
like a man losing his legs.

I tucked you in bed and kissed
your beautiful forehead.

I knew the blessing I'd found in your friendship
and it was more than the woman

who was not my fiancé
who I'd flirted with all night

and headed off to meet
at 3AM, hoping to get laid.

The Stern book was a miracle
how it put a mirror to our city

and reflected back words
we dreamed someday to write

even as we drove bridges
losing tension to old age

and walked hills
that stole our breath.

If we looked hard into our drinks
and asked to be famous

allow me to apologize
for our ignorant desires.

I have a library at home
the size of my old apartment

and we have drunk
5000 beers in the 20 years since.

The Spring of 1995 looks like a wing now
and death has been longer coming than I imagined.

So it is that two young men
from Western Pennsylvania

with fathers stuck
in factories and UPS trucks

with mothers working
in Walmart and public schools

who believed Pittsburgh
more beautiful than Paris

came to find god
inside a book of poems

written by a man with a bulldog face
who stumbled these same streets

and flicked words like matches
on paper as fine as hardwood.

Bob, I hope I tell you
I love you often enough.

Bob, you puked on my sheets that night.
I've always wanted to work that into a poem.

Gerald Stern

I wrote a poem praising Gerry Stern
          who grew up
          in Pittsburgh
          and won
the National Book Award.

I grew up 15 miles east of Pittsburgh.

I seldom dreamed of winning anything
          except for football games
          when I was a teenager

               and I certainly never dreamed
               of winning
               a National Book Award

and, even in late middle-age, it still feels
extravagant to dream of having readers.

Gerry Stern is Jewish.

I didn't think that was important
          when I wrote my poem.

When I first started reading–
and I graduated high school
without reading a poem
from the last century–

Stern's poems mattered more
     than rent
     than a decent car
     than a meal.

In the poem I called him ugly
because he's not the best-looking guy.

In the poem I called myself ugly
because I'm not the best-looking guy.

The anthology came out
and no one really noticed
     not because
     of Gerry Stern
     but because
     very few people
     care about poetry.

I got my copy and thought: yeah
     I love Gerry Stern.

But the world turns sideways, always.

Little trolls and angels work the same gig.

Weeks then months passed.

Someone said something
     about a Gerry Stern

        tribute reading
but that never happened

and I forgot about the anthology.

I went to work and did my best
        to stay in love
        with as much
        of the world
        as I could.

I wrote poems.

I read books.

My life hinged on those things.

I am so far beneath Gerry Stern
that he would have never seen the poem

except someone I knew
        knew him
        and this guy
        showed my poem
        to Stern
        thinking Stern
would love another poet
praising his brilliance

        but instead

Stern furiously dismissed my poem
and insisted I was an antisemite
         for calling him ugly.

What a twat.

PART 5

Ed Field

World War II, and Ed Field was barely a poet. He worked as a soldier flying missions over Germany, dropping bombs and taking Nazi fire, barely 20 years old and weird and a little miserable and gay and scared shitless.

America was a good place that wanted to be a great place, but good places often stink for lots of people, so America as a good place that's a mess – everyone miserable and weird and pretending not to be and lots of racists who didn't bother to pretend and most Americans neither knew nor liked anyone gay.

Terrible things were to come but great things too.

So many people wanted to save the world from Nazi Germany, a country trying to re-build itself on eugenics, antisemitism, and forced labor. A typical day in Germany started with a shot of methamphetamine, a new tank, the murder of a thousand Jews, then finished with the destruction of a neighboring country.

Ed Field was Jewish and American and unhappy in New York. He played cello in the family band. His dad raised him with beatings and without religion. Kids who were raised as Christians wanted to kick his ass for being agnostic and Jewish because they saw Jesus as a bully and not the world's sweetest Jew who preached love.

Once, Ed Field got laid at the beach, but it wasn't anything. He hitchhiked and met other gay men and snuck away to dark movie theaters to fool around. His mother loved old Jewish folk music and played the radio and encouraged her kids to be naked and dance. His father pretended not to hear the way his family passed around New World kindness like the plague.

Popular music, blech. Dancing, blech.

The talk around the house turned to careers, not poetry, not modern art. Ed Field attended college and hated the classes.

In the Air Force no one cared that he was gay. Ed Field moved into a barracks with a master sergeant and fell into a passionate affair until the affair felt a lot like hate. They drank together and brooded and swore. Romance tends to bottom out, no matter your orientation.

Ed Field aced the tests to become a fighter pilot, planning his getaway, then he quit reading Rupert Kipling.

If you're willing to drop bombs, the country will ignore who you love, even if your grand aspiration is to write poetry readable enough to be handed out in factories.

On the way to Flight School, a Red Cross worker gave Ed Field a book of poems, along with a toothbrush and a comb. One of these things felt like religion.

Then another love affair. Another plane. Endless planes.

The affair brought more poetry when Ed Field was handed TS Elliot by his new lover. Ed Field read "Prufrock" and "The Wasteland" and later said "They made no sense!"

Ed Field spent the war flying missions over Germany, 4 times shot and damaged and forced to emergency land. The 5th time he was shot, he crash-landed in the ocean and barely survived and later wrote it into a poem and many decades later that poem turned into a film. Ed Field floated in the ocean, freezing, watching other soldiers drift away and die.

Ed Field survived because Ed Field wanted to survive. He can't explain it any other way.

When the rescue boat arrived, Ed Field wept. He drank whiskey that night and re-started his combat missions a couple weeks later.

After the war but still enlisted, Ed Field saw France and England. He drank red wine and read more poetry and ate cheese and forgot to sightsee, handsome young man that he was.

Maybe someday we'll all walk into the bar and know what it means to be the attraction. Ed Field was a man to desired.

Somewhere in here Ed Field decides to become a poet. Not a hobby. Avocation. Maybe Ed Field's father was hoping for something else, but fathers are like that, and Hitler was dead in Germany.

Back in America Ed Field attended school again and skipped classes and wrote terrible poems and headed to Harlem with his black classmates. He danced. He roamed back to The Village. He signed up for a session with Dr. Kinsey when Kinsey was working on his famous study of human sexuality. Talking about sex did something, liberated something.

Ed Field quit college. More Paris. Much later, Afghanistan. Off to Greece to write poems for his first book, the most important book in the history of American poetry.

Cavafy said "And if you can't shape your life the way you want it, at least try as much as you can not to degrade it."

Ed Field said "I was obsessed with poetry but couldn't see how to survive as a poet. Getting a steady job would have meant selling out."

This is what the religious call holy.

Still, Ed Field worked in a factory. He worked in a warehouse. He read the ancient Chinese poets. He wrote more wonderful poems. He moved in with Frank O'Hara who wrote poems on his lunch break at the museum and read more William Carlos Williams, the doctor who wrote poems between visits with his patients in New Jersey.

Poems appeared in magazines. More adventures. More jobs. More reading. Ed Field wrote poems about being miserable and poems about Frankenstein and Mae West and about being gay and New York and his father and not being loved and finding love and loving poetry and he wrote his poems straight and sassy in a language so clear it appeared invisible.

Ed Field's first book *Stand Up, Friend, With Me* won the Lamont Poetry Prize and was finally published. Ed Field managed to save the stuffy world of poetry, just like he'd saved us all from the Nazis in World War II.

Marius Bewley, in *The Partisan Review*, said "Ed Field writes poems like a little girl with little curls playing Chopin in the afternoon" which actually sounds pretty fun.

But fuck off, Marius Bewley.

Ed Field is my hero.

There was poetry then there was Ed Field. Then everything changed in a way it was supposed to have changed with Whitman and William Carlos Williams but didn't.

Thanks, Ed Field.

Because of you, our poems are better and the world is a less dangerous place.

So Many of the Poets I Love

wrote about beans, maybe because they all struggled
with money, and every couple years I pull out
Gwendolyn Brooks' poems and marvel at the clarity
in the way she writes about poor black people
and the dignity of their lives and their endless struggles.
Do I dislike rhyming poems? Mostly. Do I usually
consider the sonnet a weapon? I distrust the establishment.
But sometimes the content makes the style.
Sometimes the Pulitzer Prize nods in the direction
of the downtrodden and sometimes a father will take
a job as a janitor because medical schools so seldom
accepted poor black folk. Listen to the music in her
poems if you want to understand her mother playing piano.
Gwendolyn Brooks took the story of a poor black girl
growing up in Chicago and turned her into a Greek hero.
Forgive me, I was talking about beans and endless poverty.
Gwendolyn is the thread that stitches poor black writers
through poor white writers up and into Charles Bukowski
who said about writing poetry "It's more important
than beans with garlic" though there is no poetry
without beans, without something in your stomach
and it stretches to Joan Jobe Smith who remembers
her Texas childhood and beans on the stove, how the beans
warmth "speaks to me and I understand every word."
Brooks attended a community college to learn to type
so she could make a living while learning to be a writer.
The first Brooks poem I read was at a community college.
There weren't enough copies so we had to share the pages.
Eventually, the US Government put her on a stamp, sweet
enough, but she'd already traveled the world with her words.

This Is To Say Thank You

to the mailperson who shows up 5 days a week
right around noon, lugging boxes filled with toilet
paper and paper towels and books from small presses
and books from corporate bookstores and occasionally
a letter and always a bill or a reminder to a pay a bill.
My mailperson is Judy. She wears shorts pretty much
all year, even in winter, even when it's 7 degrees out
though I once saw her with socks thick as a knit hat pulled
up and under her shorts so maybe they were tights
of some kind, insulated, made to look like old tube socks.
It's a fashion statement, delivering the mail, and a battle.
Dogs and rain and snow, and bosses who want you to lie
on your timecards and neighbors stealing packages from
other neighbors, so look good with what you're allowed.
I wave at Judy when I see her and leave 25 bucks for Xmas
and always wish I could leave 35 or 50 or 100 and maybe
I could if I weren't so greedy or worked more hours instead
of writing poems and novels and memoirs made of timeclocks.
It's tough, being loaded down like a pack animal half stuffed
with political flyers made of smoke and deception.

Judy smiles but seldom talks so I seldom talk
to respect her space and hours. I hope she's not
overwhelmed but her bag looks huge as a carny tent
and she's skinny as dental floss but must be made of wire
stretched with copper and an infinite number of miracles.

I use the word hope a lot, maybe because I don't pray, so
this is for Judy, a postcard of appreciation and respect.

I hope the life she fills with the Post Office
     allows her a second life made of joy.

May days off fall into her lap like letters from long-lost
loved ones, how they reach us through the mail that
is not the mail but something we never need to name.

Poets at the Presidential Inauguration

While lots of people discuss the value of this year's poem
read at the Presidential Inauguration, I'm just happy that
poetry has a platform that reaches people at all
and if I didn't think this year's poem was very good
I also didn't think the last Inauguration poem was very good
or any of them ever, really. It's an impossible task, writing
to reach everyone in America, to be inclusive and not offend anyone.
Probably my favorite poetry moment at a Presidential Inauguration
was Robert Frost reading for JFK, and that's only because the wind
and the glare of the sun made it impossible for him to finish the
poem he'd written especially for the occasion.

Chuck Kinder, Writer and Professor, Throws a Party

and is nice enough to invite me
but I'm not much of a party guy

especially when so many
at the party will be young people

so I stop at a bar and arrive late
and by then Professor Kinder

is surrounded by student-writers
who want to smoke his dope

and a man from West Virginia
who keeps insisting he's a doctor

and while I believe West Virginia
has as many fine doctors

as any other state in the union
including Pennsylvania

this man appears to be too drunk
and stoned to make

any sort of decisions
relating to medicine and health.

An old friend who hasn't written
a line in 20 years or more

instantly pulls me aside with a hug
like she's happy to see me

then, before I can speak, starts to explain
the book she's thinking about writing

once she finds the time
like she wants me to okay the project.

Why do I come to parties, period
let alone ones packed with writers?

I wanted to tell Chuck
I really loved his last novel

and I thought there might be someone
to talk books with, I guess

but writers mostly want to talk
about the books they're writing

not the ones they've read
if they're actually even reading

and once, years ago, a guy
wearing a beret, and I'm not joking

it was a beret
and it was tilted at a jaunty angle

said "I don't read other writers
while I'm writing

because I don't want to be
influenced by their work"

which is like a person saying
"I don't want to be around other people

while I'm breathing
because I want my breaths to be original"

but whatever
and tonight is worse:

I get stuck next to
a tenured professor

who wants to talk about
her bamboo kitchen floor

and how much her bamboo
kitchen floor costs.

I nod a lot but I'm probably
not her ideal audience.

My kitchen is 60 years old
and the cabinets are peeling apart.

She says "They're bringing
the granite counter next week."

Money seldom impresses me
nor do material possessions

except for books
and I didn't know kitchen floors

were even made of bamboo
except possibly in Asia.

My ears are made of human stuff
and it hurts to hear stupid shit.

I politely excuse myself and make
for the kitchen to grab a drink

but all the beer is gone
so I scan the counter

for what's available
which is not much.

I grab the only full bottle and decide
to mix a Makers Mark and Coke

which is about the last thing
I'd like to drink

but these nights require booze
no matter your palette.

I get about two shots of whiskey
in the glass and toss in a couple

watery ice cubes and some Coke
and stare deeply at the concoction

hoping I can turn it into a beer
with my mind

and just as I really start
to concentrate

some young fiction writer
given the illusion

that the world gives a shit
about his opinion

because nine other students
paying tuition

have been forced
to read his writing

as part of their weekly assignment
bolts across the room

in a complete tizzy
like he's just spotted

an army of cops on the front porch
and needs to hide his stash.

I assume he's making
for the back door

but he suddenly stops at the counter
and says to me

"You can't mix that with Coke!"
meaning, I guess, the Maker's Mark.

The shock on his face
and the exasperation in his voice

is so genuine and so filled
with the desire to teach and show

his knowledge of alcohol etiquette
that I take an additional second

to stir my Makers Mark and Coke
with my index finger before saying

"Get the fuck away from me."

Old Chuck, Old Hagler, Old Borges
—for Chuck Kinder

Dear Chuck, I think my wife wanted to screw you for a while
but I'm hoping it passed. She'd drink and tell the same story
about you teaching her to hit the heavy bag in your basement.
There's a man, I said about you, that has neither punched
nor been punched in 30 to 50 years. What the fuck is he doing
with a heavy bag in his basement? We all can't be Marvin Hagler
chasing motherfuckers who like to dance around the ring.
How old are you now? I hope your dick has died a natural death
and you've become the Borges we all saw reading in your heart.
Should you go blind, keep singing. The weirder, the better.
I watched the Hagler vs. Hearns fight on video at your house.
What a slugfest! I was always too poor to see the great fights
on HBO but I'd read about them in the magazine aisle
at the grocery store. Hearns broke his hand in the first round
and Hagler landed all those rights in the third so the referee
stopped the fight and everyone in your TV room cheered
and raised their glasses and a couple guys toasted joints
and inhaled like marijuana was a fine wine worth sipping.
It probably is. I'm sorry I said that about your dick.
You deserve to get laid right up until the end of days.
May your brain outlast your liver but only by seconds.
If my wife wants to sit on your face, I wish your beard
the best of luck. All great boxers have great chins.
You taught 30 years at a university, a great accomplishment
for a man who set out to rob liquor stores and write
prose like a beatnik and be a rebel like James Dean.
And: what a disappointment you've been to rebels
and bank robbers and beatniks with your teaching.

Borges said "I have always imagined that Paradise
will be a kind of library." Every book I've ever read
you've read and you've drank with half my favorite authors.
It's dangerous being stoned all the time because everyone
forgets how fucking smart you are. You never pretended
the brain was any less important than the cock or the pussy
or that the cock and pussy had purpose without a brain.
Thanks for being who you are, you wily old cunt licker.
If you go blind, see books and titties on the back
of your eyelids until death punches you into oblivion.

You wanted to be a thief and stole all our hearts.

PART 6

So Much of My Life

has been spent eating cereal
late at night, wondering how

I was going to get to sleep
when I have to be up so soon

for jobs that feel like casting
bullets to shoot at my own face.

Jack's Bar, Breakfast Time

I'd planned to drink
the night before

but ended up doing paperwork
backed by more paperwork.

I sat in the office for hours.
I complained to myself endlessly.

My boss called in the morning
and said "How'd you finish that?"

then he offered me the day off
for turning in my report early.

Gifts are miracles when you eat
your job for dinner and a midnight snack.

I said "Thanks" and drove
to the best morning bar in Pittsburgh.

I ordered a beer and shot
to honor the old men

who used to stumble from the mills
and ended up here after 3rd trick.

Hard labor often requires drink.
History is built on that fact.

I'm not sure about the rest
of our professions

because the fear is we all
start blaming our fingers

for having knuckles
and the knuckles for aching

then we end up more alcoholic
than the alcoholics that came before

but without a girder of steel
or a tall building to show for our work.

I finished my beer and shot
and ordered another beer.

The bartender said "I am so hungover"
then raised her t-shirt to fan her face.

I said "Have a drink with me"
and we did and she looked better

less pasty, more spark.
She puckered and blew me a kiss.

I don't believe in a lot
and what I believe in is mostly not

what other people believe in.

I felt blessed to be in Jack's for breakfast.

I'd brought a book to the bar.
I planned to read while I drank.

Time tipped. I drank
as much as I wanted.

The bartender went outside
to smoke and talk on her phone.

I drank my beer like I knew
it was a million dollars.

The bartender stepped inside
and said "Better, thanks"

and blew me a kiss
which I caught and blew back.

She was a kisser, the bartender.
It felt sincere but also helped with tips.

I thought I heard my last name
then someone clearly said

"Let me by you a drink!"
and touched my shoulder.

Before I could spin around
he said "Do you remember me?"

I spun and did not
but I'm bad with names and faces

mostly because the faces I see
are often not the names I'm dreaming.

I tried to remember.
I did not remember anything.

I said "It's good to see you"
and shook his hand with vigor.

I always try to lean towards kindness
because that's adulthood

all this pretend we politely
hand to each other

because we're exhausted from work
and don't want to sound like monsters.

We finished our shake.
I said "How've you been?"

He took a very long and serious breath
then turned his face

into a portrait of disappointment
that made him look like a drip

leaking through a ceiling
when you're trying to stay dry.

I was trying to figure out
how to turn back around

and get deeper into booze
and my book

when he said "You were mean to me
back in Chemistry class"

and he meant high school
some distant planet we all crash through

and, on this, my blessed
miracle of a day off

 I said "Not as mean
as I'm going to be now."

America Ends Every Day

America ends every day for someone.
In the Speedway a woman has 96 cents
on a bill of $1.01 and the cashier
looks at her like: what the fuck.
At the gas pump a man slides
his card into the reader
and the reader declines his card.
He drives to work on fumes
wondering how he'll drive home.
Across the street a cop pulls a kid
from a primered Ford Mustang
because the kid either smells
like marijuana or the cop gets
his jollies beating up poor kids.
The cop was a poor kid.
He skipped college because
he didn't want the student loans
so the police academy excluded
him because he lacked a degree
and now he makes 24 grand
 a year and uses the cop car
like a personal vehicle
because he doesn't own
a personal vehicle and his wife
wants to move into a bigger
apartment because she's pregnant.
It's not the cop's baby but the cop
doesn't know that because his wife
fell out of love last year and quit

talking to him and started sleeping
with her old high school boyfriend
who works most weekends
at his family's pizzeria but can get
away during the weekdays to screw.
The cop smashes the teenager
over the hood of his cop car.
The kid screams "I know
my rights, you fucking pig!"
and the cop bashes him again.
Someone films the whole thing.
When the cop notices the woman
with her camera, she turns and runs.
Another woman sees the clip
on a screen and says "Cops are disgusting."
She has a pretty good job and her husband
has a pretty good job and she never
thinks America ends a little every day.
After work sometimes she jogs or does yoga.
Her husband sees the clip and says
"I don't know, maybe the cop
was just doing his job" and she says
"Don't be stupid, cops are disgusting."
A cop breaking up a domestic dispute
who has never beaten anyone
hears some version of "Cops are disgusting"
almost every day and even though
he realizes he made the wrong choice
when he majored in criminal justice
he also knows he was 20 years old
and a first-time college student

at a branch campus and he needed
a major because you needed a major
to get a job and you need a job
to be alive in the world without guilt.
Sometimes he leaves his gun in the car
even though it's against protocol.
The man who supposedly hit
the woman leans against the cop
car, his hands cuffed behind his back.
The woman who called the cops
wears Christmas pajama bottoms
in July and an old ribbed tanktop
and no bra so her boobs slosh around
as she motherfucks the cop into oblivion.
She keeps coming, finger pointed.
The cops says "Would you like
me to take you to jail too?"
even though he has no intention
of taking her to jail and plans
to uncuff her boyfriend any second.
The woman says "I'd like
to see you fucking try, you pig"
and she sprints across the yard
like she's going to throw a punch
but instead stops and spits in the cop's face.
"Look at yourself" she says "You're disgusting."

The Hitman Reads "Grecian Urn" and Finally Knows He Made The Right Career Choice

Nothing quite
so beautiful
as painting
a wall
with the brains
of a yahoo
then getting
paid for the job.

That's the truth.

I Eat the Sun

Because my wife snored all night
and I had to be up at 4AM

because I write at 4AM
because I want to be a writer

and my job doesn't care about that
because my job hates poetry

and I wouldn't have slept any better
if my wife breathed in whispers

because I worry about sleep
to the point of sleeplessness

and I could not face 4AM
so I stayed in bed

and turned up my fan
to drown out the snores

snores meaning
the whole fucking world

and I wake up at 6AM
as the sun punches through the clouds

and I reshuffle my alarms
and do not want to call work

to explain I am exhausted
because everyone is exhausted

and yesterday I fell asleep
during a training

but only for 3 seconds
before my head jerked

my body to consciousness
and I immediately tried

to look alert and successful
while checking my beard for slobber

then I glanced around and saw
2 other people sound asleep

one puffing snores
from her lips like a broken train

the other with his face flat
down on his un-opened training manual

so this morning, in lieu
of starting the day

I eat the sun, all
of it in one flaming bite.

It tastes like I want
to be born again.

I go back to sleep.
My wife wakes up

and says "What
are you doing home?"

and I say
"I ate the sun"

and she says "Good
I don't have to be at work until noon"

and goes for my cock
and pretty soon is riding me

like her clitoris is both
a map and a gas pedal.

I have one of those orgasms
that tickles my eyeballs to heaven.

My boss calls and I ignore it.
The blackness outside is brutal.

Inside my house
I light everything I love

wife and kids and books
then shower to save my strength.

But crops start to die
in fields across the world.

Waves raise themselves to the heights
of skyscrapers and crash

down and turn cities
to sandy beaches and rubble

and the moon looks
like a comet gearing up for action.

I drink a couple diet Cokes
and read this from Hemingway

"I love sleep. My life has a tendency
to fall apart when I'm awake, you know"

so I go back to bed
and read some more

from a book I've read 3 times
and find this line

"A cloudy day: do you know
what that is in a town of iron works?"

Everywhere is iron works now.
Our factories are made of debt and each other.

Then my wife comes home
from her job

and says "It's really dark out there"
and sets a bottle of wine on the table.

My stomach burns
like blue flames in a circle of rocks

but also feels like a furnace
keeping the world from freezing to death

and my wife says
"Do you want to have a drink?"

knowing full well
that I do want a drink

to settle this burning
this battle between fire and dark

this battle between work and love
between tax and making art.

She brings me a beer.
I open her bottle of wine.

Maybe the time for books
has passed without my realizing it.

I work with educated people
and no one reads novels, let alone poems

but they all love zombie shows
and anything with ruffles and feathered hats.

I hold the neck of my beer bottle
like it's my cock but also

like a knife
but also like a bouquet of flowers.

I see the world and sometimes
don't know what to do

while watching people eat all
the oxygen then bowing like celebrities.

My wife moves to the dining
room table and I follow like a torch.

We could sleep but we won't.
My wife smiles and says

"I'm so happy you had the day off"
and lifts her wine in a toast.

I am happy every moment
I am allowed happiness

and many of the moments
meant to be hammersmashed.

Before I take a sip of beer
I go to the bathroom

and I lock the door
and I stand over the sink

Dave Newman

with the water running
full blast so it splashes my face

and I puke up the sun.
You're welcome and thank you.

Later, I ask my wife
to spread her pussy lips.

93

Poem from Your Guardian Angel

"I walk beside you all day and look intently at you"
–Rolf Jacobsen

If you step in front of a bus
      and lose your spleen
      and still survive
      I've succeeded.

Time is a tough equation
and there are verses for everything.

When you die, you die.

Should you live, I make money.

Days are heavenly
with a job like this.

Degrees of Genius and Wealth

I'm at work when a friend messages me
"Terrance Hayes is a genius"

so I text back
"Genius is a pretty strong word."

I attended grad school
almost 30 years ago
with Terrance Hayes
where he was a rockstar
and a little bit of a rebel
and I remember how
controversial it was
when he didn't turn
in his homework
and still got an A
in our poetry class.

My friend texts back
"No, he won a Macarthur
Genius grant."

A MacArthur Genius grant
pays something like $650,000.

That doesn't necessarily
make you a genius.

It does make you rich.

PART 7

I Was Heading to the O on Forbes Avenue in Oakland

which is the neighborhood where
the University of Pittsburgh is located

which is the school I attended that year
though the year before I attended

a community college and the year
before that another community college

and by attended I mean I sat
in classes and felt confused

while writing notes that sounded
like canaries in a coal mine.

My father worked in a factory
that made pick-up trucks.

My mother checked the hearing
of elementary school children.

In college I neither made
things nor provided care.

I took poetry classes and other
classes about rocks and dead presidents

and tried to imagine a future
while planning my death.

You can only fill a kid
with so much debt and anxiety

before they want to walk
the bridge to nothingness.

It was Friday night and I was drunk
with a bunch of friends, guys who

still attended community college
and / or worked bad jobs

and lived at home and hated
the humiliation of sleeping

in the same bed they'd slept in
since birth, all because of money.

Jobs looked like a treasure map
compared to college

and factories dying turned
the treasure map upside down.

We parked at a meter and climbed
from a dented and nicked Monte Carlo

and headed for the O
The Original Hotdog Shop

a greasy dive that served
French fries in paper boats

so large and overflowing
three people could eat themselves

sick on a large. Did they charge
extra for gravy and cheese? Yes

they did, so the world looked
terrible from almost every angle

even fun, even cheap eats
even our late-night stroll down Forbes.

Be warned: this poem ends
with cops and poetry, not fried potatoes.

I'd earned a C- the previous semester
in my Introduction to Poetry Class

or whatever the fuck it was called
but I adored the teacher, Toi Derricotte

a woman who talked a lot
about being black and from Detroit

which was confusing
because she looked white

and we were in Pittsburgh.
She referred to herself as light-skinned

and talked about her straight hair
and the rift those things caused

with dark-skinned black people
whose hair curled and kinked.

I'd never heard anyone say
light-skinned or dark-skinned

or anything about oppression
not related to money and the lack thereof.

The people I knew measured
their lives in bills and debt

which is a different kind of pain.
The people I knew had skin

that looked like they walked
through meat grinders for a living.

Toi once sang a Billie Holiday
song in the middle of class

like it was a lecture
and her voice vibrated

with so much feeling
with so much ache

I put my face in my hands
but casually so no one would see

me cry if I cried and I definitely
cried because art

because song, because poetry
because twice after class Toi asked

if I planned to kill myself
which I absolutely planned to do

but which I felt less like doing
in the presence of her voice

which sounded like a jazz song
a breath of concern and community.

Another thing she asked
with equal weight

was "Who do you read?" like books
might be the antidote to death.

I shrugged because the answer
was no one and the textbook

we used in class bored me
and sometimes the words rhymed.

The world outside never rhymed.
The world made its own music.

Three blocks from The O
straight down Forbes Avenue

sat a used bookstore.
It was mostly self-help paperbacks

arranged on folding card tables
like an abandoned city.

I walked there with purpose
because I wanted to be reading

because I'd finally been asked
who I was reading and now

I knew I should have been reading
and I wanted to read, desperately

like how those TV preachers
healed sinners with a touch.

I wanted to be saved.
I wanted to be a savior.

I dug into the poetry section
and it looked like hieroglyphics

or maybe books of poetry
because I'd never read, not poetry

not really, just the assignments
in class and at home I'd read

the Bible and devotionals
because I'd been forced

to attend church
and forced to read

church stuff which sounded
like fantasy, a man surviving

in a lions' den, another man
slaying thousands with the jaw

of a donkey, a 100-year-old
woman giving birth to a child

but now I stood
in the poetry section, pulling

and replacing and trying to focus
and pulling and replacing

and I shit you not
I picked a book because

it was blurbed by Dear Abby
who was famous for offering

romantic and practical advice
in a nationally syndicated column

which read like a candle
lit by your great aunt with bad breath.

But back to Forbes Avenue and The O.
I was medium drunk but super hungry.

I think we'd been smoking dope.
Maybe it was more. Drugs answered

more questions than my classes
and cost a lot less than tuition.

It was late. Most of the city's drunks
had found mattresses or floors

but we walked with purpose
and I kept wondering if I had enough

money to afford cheese or gravy
because ketchup was great but nothing

as tasteful as cheese or gravy.
I would have built my life

around cheese and gravy
if I could have afforded it.

But money. But poetry.
But late night with no chicks.

Those were my three thoughts
as I walked up Forbes Avenue

lagging, dreaming my dreams
when this frat dude in a frat jacket

walking with his frat pals in frat jackets
planted his shoulder into my chest

so hard he spun me like a top
which forced me to walk backwards

to keep from landing on my ass.
The frat guy said "You want

some of this?" and started
his own backstep, waving for me

to come on, his buddies taunting
in their frat guy ways

tugging on their frat guy jackets.
I turned to my buddies

who were almost to the O
oblivious to anything but munchies.

I really did not feel like fighting
which is how I'd been feeling

about college and studying and life:
the effort may not be worth the results.

The results appeared to be endless
student loan debt and a job

selling things no one wanted.
I knew a dude going house to house

begging people to buy windows.
I'd eventually end up selling

windows and driving truck
and painting houses and caring for the sick

but now the frat guy flipped me off
and stopped and took off his frat jacket

in a very dramatic way
almost a dance, a boxer in a ring

so I touched my pal Pat
and said "I'm gonna go

knock this guy out"
which sounded better than suicide

but maybe not as great
as learning the trade of poetry.

I didn't wait around for Pat's response
or to see if he even heard my voice.

I started back down Forbes Avenue
away from The O and farther away

from the used bookstore where I'd bought
There are Men Too Gentle to Live Among Wolves

based on Dear Abby's recommendation.
I'd read the book in one sitting and knew

it was terrible, like babbling sermon terrible
with lines like "But you, Maria, sacred whore

on the endless pavement of pain"
but I loved it anyway, for the words

the way they lined up like trains
rolling down tracks to some distant light

just as I was rolling down Forbes Avenue
hoping for light, meaning victory.

The frat guy strutted and bobbed
and sang "Come on, big man."

So I came on, three big steps
and threw a roundhouse at his head

like I wanted to remake his face
with dents and blood, and it landed

and he dropped like he'd been meaning
to take a nap right there

on Forbes Avenue, the Cathedral of Learning
less than a block away

a building named after
the religion of education

but owned by a corporation
charging thousands to learn.

I took all my poetry classes
in the Cathedral of Learning

and I sometimes rocked
at my desk, filled with language

filled with desire to be something
I'd never known anyone to be.

A week after this, Toi Derricotte pulled
me aside after class and handed me a book.

A week after this, when I'd already read
There are Men Too Gentle to Live Among Wolves

3 or 4 more times, studying lines
like "I played God today! It was fun!"

which was straight-up puke
but which I wrapped around

my brain like rope I could climb
to somehow leave the world

of bad jobs and worse debt
and endless violence.

I believed in rope.
I always saw myself as climbing.

I always saw myself
as falling from every height.

When my mother said God
would come back and lift

the believers through the sky
and I knew I was not a believer

I made a plan to grab
the rope of my mom's legs

as she floated to Heaven
so that I too could find the glory

but my mom said God wouldn't allow
sinners to be pulled up by believers.

When Toi Derricotte handed me
a copy of *What Work Is*

a beautiful burgundy hardback
with a factory worker on the cover

a girl too young to be a factory worker
I thanked her profusely and walked

to the nearest lamp and sat
and the poems read like cars being assembled

and I knew everyone, every character
the firemen and waitresses and line workers.

I knew the factories.
I knew the uniforms and gloves

and the marks on the skins
of everyone who stepped into fire.

I wrote fifty poems that week
burning up the cross

where experience hangs with language
hangs with imagery, hangs with meaning

and, more importantly, one of the frat guy's
friends said "What the fuck, man?"

alternatively staring at me then staring
at his pal stretched out on the pavement

then he tried to shove me and missed
and spun back and I punched him

and, more importantly, another frat guy
said "What the fuck, man?"

and my friends showed up running
and started fighting with everyone

sort of like the Socs and the Greasers
in *The Outsiders*, a book I'd stolen

from the mall in 6th grade
and which my mom rolled

her eyes at, meaning: don't read that book
and meaning: the only book is the Bible.

The fighting on Forbes Avenue continued
so I heard punches landing

like balls in a catcher's mitt
like birds crashing into windows.

Then two cops appeared on foot
their uniforms blue as the ocean at night

and they started shouting
and they started shoving

and they wore hats
with badges above their brims.

I got frat-punched
but was too hyped to feel it.

The guy I knocked out
wobbled back up and stumbled

into a cop, accidentally but hard
and the cop grabbed him

in some sort of hold
a sort of mid-body choke

and the kid instinctively started to swing
and the cop clamped down

so he trapped the kid's arms
so they pointed skyward like kites

and his shirt was up
and his ribs were exposed

and the cop said "He went for my gun!"
and the other cop instantly started

banging his billyclub on the kid's ribs
and my pal Pat said "Run!"

and we all did, both groups.
I booked ass straight

for the Cathedral of Learning
which looked like a brick dick

shining spotlights from 50 floors
so I ducked right and sprinted

past the museum and the library
places I knew but didn't know

a world I wanted to explore
but not now, obviously

then hung another right, past
the home plate from old Forbes Field

and ended up on McKee Street
in my shitty college apartment

out of breath, out of beer
my friends stumbling in

all of us scared but maybe
exhilarated but mostly scared

of cops and jail
and of falling in the street.

Nobody said anything then someone
said "You see the cop beat that kid?"

We all nodded.
We saw exactly what we knew.

You want to see your life in miniature
take a close look at a billyclub moving

at the speed of bees wings
on some kid's ribs and spine.

For years after this I walked past
the library and the museum

and the room where the Pittsburgh Cultural Trust
hosts the Pittsburgh Arts & Lecture series

and I thought: how can I be a part of that?
The answer was, of course, I couldn't.

They didn't let people like me in.
They still don't. That's okay.

I read every single day.
I taught myself to write books.

Acknowledgements

Some of these poems appeared in the following magazines, usually in different forms, sometimes with different titles. Thanks to the editors.

Misfit
Nerve Cowboy
5AM
Chiron Review

Some of these poems also appeared in the chapbook *Allen Ginsberg Comes To Pittsburgh* and the anthology *Poems For Jerry* published by John Schulman and Caliban Bookshop.

Thanks to Louie Ickes for his wonderful painting that graces the cover of this book. Love you, Louie!

Thanks to David Conrad for the acting, the writing, and the introduction to this book. I owe you wine, brisket, and a piece of furniture to set on fire. Please start wearing socks.

Thanks to Lori Jakiela for everything, always. We wrote our way to this. What a fucking blessing.

Dave Newman is the author of nine books, including the story collection *She Throws Herself Forward to Stop the Fall* (Roadside Press, 2024) and *How to Live Like Li Po in Pittsburgh: essays from a writing life* (J.New Books, 2024). His collection *The Slaughterhouse Poems* (White Gorilla Press, 2013) was named one of the best books of the year by *L Magazine*. He was a finalist for the Rattle Poetry Prize and won the Readers' Choice Award in 2024. His poems, essays, and stories have appeared in magazines and journals around the world, including *Ambit* (U.K.), *Tears In The Fence* (U.K.), *Gulf Stream, Belt,* and the legendary *Nerve Cowboy*. He appeared in the PBS documentary narrated by Rick Sebak about Pittsburgh writers. Winner of numerous awards, including the Andre Dubus Novella Prize, he lives in Trafford, PA, the last town in the Electric Valley, with his wife, the writer Lori Jakiela. After a decade of working in medical research, he currently teaches in the Creative and Professional Writing Program at The University of Pittsburgh-Greensburg, his alma mater.

MORE ROADSIDE PRESS TITLES